LITTLE CITIZENS

WE TAKE TURNS

THERESA EMMINIZER

PowerKiDS
press.

Published in 2023 by The Rosen Publishing Group, Inc.
2544 Clinton St, Buffalo, NY 14224

First Edition

Editor: Theresa Emminizer
Book Design: Rachel Rising

Photo Credits: Cover, p. 1 Inside Creative House/Shutterstock.com; pp. 4, 6, 8, 10, 12, 14, 18, 20 somen/Shutterstock.com; p. 5 GagliardiPhotography/Shutterstock.com; p. 7 Altrendo Images/Shutterstock.com; p. 9 LightField Studios/Shutterstock.com; pp.11, 13 Sunflower Light Pro/Shutterstock.com; p. 15 Anant Jadhav/Shutterstock.com; p. 17 imagedb.com/Shutterstock.com; p. 19 lovedv/Shutterstock.com; p. 21 Rawpixel.com/Shutterstock.com.

Some of the images in this book illustrate individuals who are models. The depictions do not imply actual situations or events.

Library of Congress Cataloging-in-Publication Data
Names: Emminizer, Theresa.
Title: We Take Turns / Theresa Emminizer.
Description: New York : Powerkids Press, 2023. | Series: Little Citizens | Includes glossary and index.
Identifiers: ISBN 9781538389263 (pbk.) | ISBN 9781538389287 (library bound) | ISBN 9781538389294 (ebook)
Subjects: LCSH: Citizen participation–Juvenile literature. | Communication–Juvenile literature. | Conduct of Life–Juvenile literature. | Sharing–Juvenile literature.
Classification: LCC BJ1533.G4 E46 2023 | DDC 177/.7 –dc23

Manufactured in the United States of America

CPSIA Compliance Information: Batch #CWPK23. For Further Information contact Rosen Publishing, New York at 1-800-237-9932.

Find us on

CONTENTS

Be a Good Citizen

You belong to a community. You're a member of your country. You're a **citizen**! Citizens have **rights**. We also have **responsibilities**. We need to act a certain way for the good of everyone. Good citizens take turns.

Taking Turns Matters

Taking turns is important. It keeps us safe. Just think, if cars didn't wait their turn at stop signs, it would be very **dangerous**! Taking turns helps us have fun too. We can practice taking turns in small ways every day.

Taking Turns Talking

Taking turns is a big part of communicating, or sharing thoughts and ideas. We take turns when we talk to each other. We don't **interrupt**. Otherwise, it's very hard to listen and understand what someone is trying to say!

Turn-Taking in Action

Sharing time is Elle's favorite part of the school day. She and her classmates sit in a big circle on the floor. Their teacher Ms. Vail asks everyone to share something interesting that they did or saw that week.

The children pass a ball around the circle. When someone is holding the ball, it's their turn to talk! As the ball moves closer to Elle, she gets very excited. But she sits still and quiet until it's her turn to talk.

13

Fun Taking Turns

Taking turns is a key part of playing together. At the playground, sometimes we have to wait our turn before playing with something. Think how you'd feel if someone was hogging the slide. It's much more fun when we all take turns.

Turn-Taking in Action

Stevie is playing a game with her friend Nate. But Nate isn't taking turns. Nate makes move after move. He's winning, but it isn't fair. Stevie feels mad. She takes a deep breath. She tells Nate it's *her* turn to play.

If someone isn't letting you take your turn, it's okay to speak up about it! Sometimes people get so caught up having fun that they forget to take turns. When that happens, we can remind them kindly. We can start over.

Take Your Turn!

Taking turns shows **respect**. It honors a person's time and feelings. You're worthy of your turn being honored. Others are too! By taking turns we can make our community a better, fairer, and more respectful place for everybody.

GLOSSARY

citizen: One who lives in a country legally and has certain rights.

dangerous: Unsafe.

interrupt: To stop by breaking in.

respect: A feeling of understanding and caring about someone's wishes and well-being.

responsibility: Something a person is in charge of.

right: Something someone is allowed to have, get, or do by law.

FOR MORE INFORMATION

BOOKS

Adams, Kenneth. *Sharing with Others.* New York, NY: PowerKids Press, 2022.

Adams, Kenneth. *Listening to Others.* New York, NY: PowerKids Press, 2022.

WEBSITES

Britannica Kids

kids.britannica.com/kids/article/citizenship/399912
Read more about how you can be a better citizen!

PBS

www.pbs.org/parents/crafts-and-experiments/my-turn-a-simple-game-about-taking-turns
Ask a grown up to help you play this game about taking turns!

INDEX